Jaguar XK

by Julie Wilson

AXIS education

Acknowledgements

Cover design: Oliver Heath, Rafters Design

Photographs © Ford Motor Company

Copyright © Axis Education 2005

First published in Great Britain by Axis Education Ltd

ISBN 1-84618-010-4

Axis Education
PO Box 459
Shrewsbury
SY4 4WZ

Email: enquiries@axiseducation.co.uk

www.axiseducation.co.uk

This is a fast car.

It is a Jaguar XK.

It is smart.

It looks great.

The 2004 Jaguar XK.

Jaguar is a car maker.

It has made cars for many years.

It began in 1922.

It has made sports cars since 1936.

The 1949 Jaguar XK120.

There are different models of the Jaguar XK.

The XKR is a sporty Jaguar.

It is not as heavy as other Jaguars.

It is made of carbon panels.

The car is made of carbon.

The XK is a sporty Jaguar.

The XK looks smart.

A trendy car!

The XK is elegant.

It is curvy.

It looks sleek.

It looks trendy.

The Jaguar XK is a sleek car.

Jaguar makes six XK models.

There are three coupes.

These are the XK, XKR and XK8.

They also make a convertible.

These are the XK, XKR and XK8.

They cost between £50,000 and £72,000.

Jaguar XK models.

The XK Convertible.

The XK Coupe.

The Jaguar XK is good to drive.

The gears are easy to use.

The steering feels easy.

It holds when you go round bends.

Going round the bend.

Inside you are in the lap of luxury.

The seats are made of leather.

They get hot if you want.

You can move them forward and back.

The seats in the XK can get hot.

The XK has real wood trims.

These have been hand-polished.

It has a leather steering wheel.

The steering wheel can go up or down to fit.

The wood is hand-polished.

Each model has headlamps that turn themselves on.

They know when it's dark.

The headlamps have wipers that turn on when it rains.

You don't have to do anything.

The headlamps know when it's dark.

The XK helps you to park.

It knows if you are about to hit something.

It bleeps to let you know.

This saves your bumper!

The XK can tell if you are about to hit something.

The wing mirrors can fold in.

This also helps when you are parking.

They heat up in the cold.

They don't mist up in the rain.

The wing mirrors can fold in.

The CD player can take six CDs.

It is easy to stack.

There are six speakers.

You can even get an XK with a phone!

Six speakers and six CDs!

You can get an XK with a phone.

It looks great on the road.

You get a buzz from driving the Jaguar XK.

You turn heads in this car.

People dream of having a Jaguar.

It grips the road.

The stuff of dreams.

The Jaguar XK has been in films.

Austin Powers has an XK8.

He calls it the 'Shaguar'.

It is his secret weapon.

Even Austin Powers wants one!

The Jaguar XK is very fast.

It can go up to 155 miles per hour

(249 kilometres per hour).

It can go from 0 to 62 miles per hour

(0 to 100 kilometres per hour) in 5 seconds.

You drive like the wind in an XK.

The XK can go from 0 to 62 miles per hour (0 to 100 kilometres per hour) in 5 seconds.

Technical specification – *Jaguar XKR Coupe*

Make	Jaguar
Model	XKR Coupe
Engine size	4196cc
Top speed	155mph (249kmh)
Acceleration	0–60mph (0–100kmh) in 5 seconds
Fuel tank capacity	75 litres
Price	£60,000
Weight	1735kg
Transmission	6-speed automatic
Wheelbase	2588mm
Tyres	F 245/50 ZR 17, R 245/50 ZR 17

Glossary

acceleration	how fast the car speeds up
bleep	a high-pitched sound
capacity	how much petrol the engine can hold
carbon	a metal some cars are made of
cc (cubic centimetres)	a measure of engine capacity
convertible	a car with a roof you can put down
coupe	a car with a fixed roof, two doors, two or four seats, and usually a sloping back
curvy	wavy, rounded
dream	to hope for something you think you will never get
elegant	smart, neat
gears	a set of small wheels that control how much power from the engine goes to make the car move
great	good, cool
hand-polished	made smooth and shiny by rubbing with a cloth
heat	warmth
heavy	solid, strong, not light
kg (kilogram)	a measure of weight (just over 2 pounds)
km (kilometre)	a measure of distance (just over half a mile)
kmh	kilometres per hour
leather	the skin of a cow

litre	a measure of liquid (just under 2 pints)
luxury	posh comfort
make	the name of the car maker
mm (millimetre)	a small measure of length: 10mm = 1cm (centimeter)
mph	miles per hour
panels	large pieces of metal
per	for every
phone	short for telephone
rain	water from the sky
secret weapon	something that no one knows about that gives you an edge over others
sleek	smooth and shiny
smart	cool, trendy, good-looking
speakers	boxes that play the sound from a CD or radio
steering	using the steering wheel to take the car where you want to go
transmission	another word for gearbox
trendy	in fashion, cool
trims	frills, edges
wheelbase	the distance between the front and rear wheels
wing mirrors	the side mirrors